THIS WALKER BOOK BELONGS TO:

_____

_____

_____

_____

First published individually as
Dad's Back, Messy Baby,
Reading and *Sleeping*
in 1985 by Walker Books Ltd
87 Vauxhall Walk, London SE11 5HJ

This edition published 1998

10 9 8 7 6 5 4 3 2 1

This book has been typeset in Bembo Educational.

Printed in Hong Kong

British Library Cataloguing in Publication Data
A catalogue record for this book is
available from the British Library.

ISBN 0-7445-6302-X

DAD AND ME

JAN ORMEROD

WALKER BOOKS

AND SUBSIDIARIES

LONDON • BOSTON • SYDNEY

Contents

Playing *6*
Reading *12*
Sleeping *16*
Messy Baby *18*

Playing

Dad's back with jingling keys,
warm gloves, a cold nose ...

a long, long scarf
and apples in a bag.

9

Dad's back with a game,

a chase

and a tickle.

Reading

climbing over

crawling under

pushing through,
climbing up

relaxing

13

peeping over

reading

Sleeping

peeping

tickling

climbing up

bouncing

pulling his nose

cuddling

17

Messy Baby

Dad says,

    "Soft toys in the box."

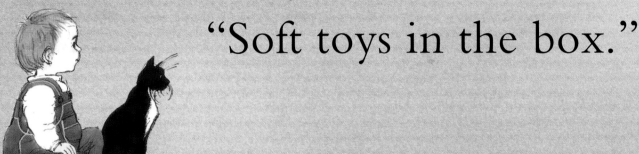

18

He says,

"Books on the shelf."

19

Dad says, "Clothes in the cupboard.

He says, "Rubbish in the basket.

Bricks in the cart."

Food off the floor."

"Oh no, what a mess!
Oh, you messy baby!"

"Never mind," Dad says.
"Let's start again."

MORE WALKER PAPERBACKS
For You to Enjoy

Also by Jan Ormerod

MUM AND ME

This book contains four simple, beautifully observed studies of the special relationship between a mother and a young child.

"Gentle, humorous and true to life… Recommended for the youngest child." *The Times Educational Supplement*

0-7445-6010-1   £4.50

EAT UP, GEMMA

written by Sarah Hayes, illustrated by Jan Ormerod

A story about the food exploits of baby Gemma, the youngest member of a Black English family.

"Great child appeal, accurately reflecting the warmth of family life." *Books for Keeps*

0-7445-1328-6   £4.99

WHEN WE WENT TO THE ZOO

"Wonderful animal pictures … the book as a whole adds up to a great experience for a child."
Tony Bradman, Parents

0-7445-2318-4   £4.99

Walker Paperbacks are available from most booksellers, or by post from B.B.C.S., P.O. Box 941, Hull, North Humberside HU1 3YQ

24 hour telephone credit card line 01482 224626

To order, send: Title, author, ISBN number and price for each book ordered, your full name and address, cheque or postal order payable to BBCS for the total amount and allow the following for postage and packing:
UK and BFPO: £1.00 for the first book, and 50p for each additional book to a maximum of £3.50.
Overseas and Eire: £2.00 for the first book, £1.00 for the second and 50p for each additional book.

Prices and availability are subject to change without notice.